THE
FIFTY-MINUTE
SUPERVISOR

THE
FIFTY-MINUTE
SUPERVISOR

A Guide for the Newly Promoted

Elwood N Chapman

KOGAN
PAGE

First published in the United States of America
in 1986 by Crisp Publications Inc, 95 First Street,
Los Altos, California 94022, USA

This edition first published in Great Britain in
1988 by Kogan Page Ltd, 120 Pentonville Road,
London N1 9JN

Reprinted 1989

British Library Cataloguing in Publication Data

Chapman, Elwood N.
    The fifty-minute supervisor.
    1. Personal management
    I. Title
    658.3

    ISBN 1-85091-645-4
    ISBN 1-85091-641-1 Pbk

Typeset by DP Photosetting, Aylesbury, Bucks
Printed and bound in Great Britain by
Dotesios (Printers) Ltd, Bradford-on-Avon, Wiltshire

Contents

Preface

Improving the quality of first line supervision has always been considered essential by successful executives because of the immediate impact on employee productivity. As a result, training directors allocate a sizable portion of their budget to new supervisor training. A common problem, however, has been that because of factors such as geographical dispersion, or the time of year, considerable time may elapse before a new supervisor receives help. This can lead to costly mistakes or the formation of poor habits before formal training takes place. *The Fifty-Minute Supervisor* was developed to remedy this training delay problem.

To the Reader

Congratulations on becoming a supervisor. In approximately 50 minutes you will know many secrets of good supervision. What you learn, and any positive changes you make in your behaviour, are far more important than the time it takes to finish, so please *do not read so fast that you miss something*.

To benefit fully, be honest, especially when you rate yourself on factors such as attitude and self-confidence. It is not what you are now, but what you can become as a successful supervisor that will help you progress in your organisation.

Elwood N Chapman

CHAPTER 1
Successes and Failures

As you contemplate making your transition into a supervisory role, it is often a good idea to model your behaviour on a successful supervisor you respect.

You will discover that highly successful supervisors have much in common. If the opportunity presents itself, discuss some of the characteristics and principles of good supervision with your manager. Some of these characteristics are presented below.

Make your choice now

Successful supervisors
Those who build and maintain mutually rewarding relationships with their employees.

Supervisors who learn to set reasonable and consistent authority lines.

Those who learn to delegate.

Those who establish standards of high quality and set good examples.

Individuals who work hard to become good communicators.

Leaders who build team effort to achieve high productivity.

Add your own:

_____

_____

_____

Supervisors who fail

Individuals insensitive to employee needs.

Those not interested in learning the basic supervisory skills.

Those who fail to understand it is not what a supervisor can do but what supervisors can get others to accomplish that is important.

Supervisors who let their status go to their heads.

Those who become either too authoritarian or too lax.

Add your own:

_____

_____

_____

As an employee, you have had the opportunity to study mistakes supervisors make. List three you do not intend to make.

1. _____

2. _____

3. _____

Many new, inexperienced supervisors enjoy setting success goals for themselves. A good way to do this is to identify, discuss, and refine such goals with your immediate superior and then ask this person to monitor your progress for a 30-day period.

CHAPTER 2
Who Will Survive?

A case study is designed to provide insights you may not possess. Four case problems are included in this book.

The case below will help you to understand some of the things involved in making the transition to a successful supervisor.

Case 1

Assume that Joe and Mary are equally qualified to take on the role of supervisor in the same department. Further assume that they adopt different attitudes towards their new challenge. Which one, in your opinion, stands the best chance of surviving after six months?

Joe received news of his promotion by throwing a party for his close friends. Although he received two weeks' advance notice, he did little to prepare for the new assignment. Joe reckoned he had worked under enough supervisors to know what to do. He would model his behaviour on what he had learned from observation. Why bother to study techniques and principles in advance? Why get stressed needlessly by too much preparation? Joe believes that personality and good common sense are all that is needed.

His only strategy will be to set a good example by personally working hard, staying close to the group and doing a lot of listening. Joe has complete confidence in his ability to succeed.

Mary was delighted with the announcement of her promotion. She decided to use the two-week period to prepare for her new responsibilities. She quickly found some good books on supervision and started to make a list of recommended techniques to follow. How to demonstrate authority? When to delegate? What changes in behaviour would be required etc? Mary accepted the premise that she had much to learn about becoming a successful supervisor. Although she believes in herself, she does not have Joe's level of confidence.

Mary has decided on the following strategy. Although she intends to remain friendly, she will slowly pull back from too much personal contact with former fellow-employees. She feels this will be necessary to demonstrate her authority. Next she will concentrate on creating a good working environment so that workers are more relaxed. Everything will be planned and orderly. Everyone will know where they stand and what is expected.

Which individual has the best chance of survival? Will Joe with his outgoing, confident approach do a better job than Mary with her more scientific attitude? Or will Mary, with her less confident but more deliberate strategy, overtake Joe? Tick the appropriate box below and compare your decision with that of the author on page 63.

☐ Joe will survive.

☐ Mary will survive.

☐ Both Joe and Mary will survive.

CHAPTER 3
What Can Success as a Supervisor Do for You?

Is supervision *really* for you?

Some people are happy and effective as supervisors; others are not. Now is the time to discover whether management is for you. Complete the activity below to see if you are in agreement with the advantages of being a successful supervisor.

Many good things can happen to you once you become a successful supervisor. Ten statements are listed below. Three are false. Tick the square opposite the false statements and match your answers with those on page 14.

As a supervisor you will:

☐ 1. Increase your earnings potential.

☐ 2. Have opportunities to learn more.

☐ 3. Develop an ulcer.

☐ 4. Position yourself for promotion to higher management.

☐ 5. Have less freedom.

☐ 6. Increase your self-confidence.

☐ 7. Try out your leadership wings.

☐ 8. Have fewer friends.

☐ 9. Learn and develop human relations skills.

☐ 10. Have better feelings of self worth.

False statements on page 13

3. There is no evidence that supervisors have more ulcers than non-supervisors.

5. Supervisors normally have more freedom because they control their actions more than employees do.

8. Good supervisors develop new friends and keep the old ones.

CHAPTER 4
Your Attitude to Being a Supervisor

Attitude is the way you look at things *mentally*. You have the power to look at your new position in any way you wish. If you look at it in a positive, enthusiastic manner you will communicate to your employees that you are ready to accept your new responsibility and they will enjoy working for you. If you are tentative or insecure they may interpret your attitude as negative and you may receive less cooperation.

As a new supervisor, you will be watched by everyone and no matter what you may do to hide it, your attitude will show.

If you have not already done so, now is an ideal time to read a book entitled *How to Develop a Positive Attitude* (Kogan Page). This simple publication will provide the human relations foundation you need to become a superior supervisor.

To measure your attitude, complete this exercise. Read each statement and circle the number where you feel you belong. If you circle a 5, you are saying your attitude could not be better in this area; if you circle a 1, you are saying supervision may not be for you.

	Agree			Disagree	
I seek responsibility.	5	4	3	2	1
Becoming a respected supervisor is important to me.	5	4	3	2	1
I enjoy helping others do a good job.	5	4	3	2	1
I want to know more about human behaviour.	5	4	3	2	1
I want to climb the management ladder.	5	4	3	2	1
I am anxious to learn and master supervisory skills.	5	4	3	2	1

I like leadership situations.   5   4   3   2   1

Working with a problem employee would
be an interesting challenge.   5   4   3   2   1

I intend to devote time to learning
motivational skills.   5   4   3   2   1

I'm excited about the opportunity to
become a supervisor.   5   4   3   2   1

TOTAL

If you scored above 40, you have an excellent attitude to becoming a supervisor. If you rated yourself between 25 and 40, it would appear you have a few reservations. A rating under 25 indicates you probably should not pursue becoming a supervisor.

Nothing will improve relationships with those you supervise more than a consistently positive attitude. *Your* attitude sets the pace and the tone in your department. If you are late arriving at work, it will be reflected in the attitudes of your staff; if you discuss the negative aspects of your organisation with employees, your comments will eventually be reflected in their attitudes. In fact *everything you do and every position you take will be reflected in the attitudes of your employees.* As you study the attitudes on the following pages, keep in mind that ATTITUDES ARE CAUGHT – NOT TAUGHT!

Do you recognise any of these attitudes?

My supervisor is usually late, so why should I be on time?
If my boss says things are bad, they must be.
Don't ask me ... I just work here.

Every time I try something new I am shouted at, so why try? Only 31½ years until retirement.

When you are negative your team will show these attitudes and their productivity will fall.

CHAPTER 5
Self-confidence Scale

Along with a positive attitude, it takes personal confidence to become a successful supervisor. This exercise is designed to help you discover your level of self-confidence. Read the statement and circle the number where you feel you belong.

	Agree				*Disagree*
I'm not easily intimidated.	5	4	3	2	1
Complex problems do not overwhelm me.	5	4	3	2	1
If necessary, I can discipline those who require it.	5	4	3	2	1
I can make a decision and stick to it.	5	4	3	2	1
I am strong enough to defend a deserving employee with a superior.	5	4	3	2	1
I have enough confidence to be a good teacher.	5	4	3	2	1
Speaking in public does not frighten me.	5	4	3	2	1
Superiors are basically people like me.	5	4	3	2	1
I won't avoid confrontations, when required.	5	4	3	2	1
I can say 'NO' when necessary.	5	4	3	2	1

TOTAL

If you scored 40 or above on both attitude and self-confidence, you have a winning combination as far as being a successful supervisor is concerned. If you scored lower on self-confidence than attitude, it is a signal that you need to learn to take a firmer stand on those items relating to supervision.

When you first start out, like others, you may not have *all* the confidence you would like, but *do not lose faith in yourself*. As a supervisor, you will slowly build your level of personal confidence. That is one of the advantages of becoming a supervisor in the first place.

As you work on this goal, keep in mind that you need not be a highly verbal extrovert to be successful. Quiet, sensitive people become excellent supervisors even though they may not show their personal confidence on the outside.

CHAPTER 6
Convert to a Stronger Image

Supervisors are 'in-charge' people. As leaders, they use their sources of power in sensitive but effective ways. When you assume your role as a supervisor-leader, you have three sources of power to tap:

First you have 'knowledge' because of what you know about the department you lead. In most cases, you *know* more than those who work for you. When you teach them what you know, you make the best use of your 'knowledge power'.

Second, you gain power from the role you occupy. Just being the supervisor gives you authority which you must use gently and wisely.

Third, you have 'personality power'. You can persuade or motivate others through your positive attitude, friendly manner, patience and other personal characteristics.

Although you must be sensitive in the way you use your power (do not let your new position go to your head), properly used, the three sources of power can help you to become the kind of supervisor you want to be.

It is important that a new supervisor learns to communicate a 'take charge' image. She or he must let everyone know (co-workers and superiors) that things are under control – that decisions are being made and that the role of supervisor is comfortable. All this must be accomplished without giving an impression that the new position has gone to the individual's head. It must be a natural transition.

Why is a stronger image necessary? Among other reasons, your employees want you to be a leader. They will produce more if they know they are part of a cohesive group with established standards. In contrast, a weak supervisor will cause employees to be confused and unproductive.

How do you communicate a stronger image? Here are some suggestions. Tick the square if you agree.

☐ *Improve your appearance.* Don't overdo it but look the part. Dress for success.

☐ *Make firm decisions.* In making decisions, do it with confidence. Demonstrate you can handle decision-making.

☐ *Set a faster tempo.* Move about with more energy. Become a model of productivity.

☐ *Handle mistakes calmly.* When things go wrong, collect the facts, and develop a solution. Show your inner strength.

☐ *Share humorous incidents.* Balance your authority with a sense of humour. Help everyone to have a little fun.

☐ *Demonstrate your ability to communicate with superiors.* Employees will feel more secure and produce more when they know you can represent them.

☐ *Be a positive person.* Stay in touch with members of your team in a positive manner. Keep in mind that their positive attitudes are dependent upon yours.

CHAPTER 7
Demonstrate Your Authority and Style

Establishing and maintaining fair, open, and healthy relationships with all employees is the key to good supervision. This includes the establishment of authority or a *discipline line*. This line is a well-defined, well-communicated set of behaviour standards that you expect all employees to maintain. It tells an employee what is expected and what is not permitted.

Most employees enjoy working in an environment that has high but achievable standards. They feel more secure about their jobs when their supervisor is an 'in-charge' person who does not permit one employee to 'get away' with recognised violations.

It is important to set a reasonable and *consistent* discipline line. As you learn to do this, keep in mind that there is nothing incompatible about showing compassion and maintaining high standards at the same time.

First you must demonstrate that you are in charge and know what you are doing. You need to establish a style of your own. As you do this, give your team time to adjust. You are more interested in long-term, sustainable productivity than immediate results that may not last. This means the establishment of a sound working relationship with your employees.

In making your transition, consider these tips:

1. Set high (but attainable) standards at the outset. The lower your standards at the beginning, the more difficult it will be to improve productivity later.
2. Make an effort to establish a good relationship with each individual employee as soon as practicable. This means working to get to know each employee personally and letting them know you care. It is not a sign of weakness to show understanding. You can be a sensitive supervisor and still be a disciplinarian.
3. Quickly rebuke those who are not meeting your standards, so they have no doubts about what is expected.

4. Keep in mind that a few important standards (or rules) are better than a list of complicated directions. Do not be a 'picky' supervisor. Instead, set basic terms that all understand and can attain.

Nothing undermines your authority faster than playing favourites. Employees need to be treated equally – especially if some are personal friends.

Setting the right discipline line

As you become a supervisor you must draw a discipline line that employees understand. The establishment of a framework of values will allow your employees to operate securely. Supervisors must set discipline lines based upon their own, special work environment and individual style.

CHAPTER 8
Which Strategy Should Henry Use?

Case 2

Although sensitive to the needs of fellow-workers, Henry has always set higher standards for himself. He is never late, seldom absent and, once on the job, all business. Henry attributes his work style to his upbringing and religious training. Henry is respected more by management than fellow employees.

Yesterday Henry was promoted to supervisor of his own department. When they informed him of the promotion, Henry's superiors said: 'You were selected because we think you can put some discipline back into the department. As you know, your department is a mess, but we think you can clean it up. It won't be easy, but we have faith in you, Henry.'

Last night Henry sat down and developed three different strategies to consider. Which one would you recommend Henry to employ?

Strategy 1
Set a good example and give employees time to adjust to it.

Strategy 2
Call a departmental meeting and, in a low-key manner explain the mission you have been given by your superiors. Explain that the higher standards you will impose will not only protect their jobs in the future but will give them more pride in what they are doing now. Tell them you will be hard but fair.

Strategy 3
Do the same as strategy 2 but on an individual counselling basis. Call in each person and explain the changes that will be made and why.

Write out your answer below.

I would recommend Henry to employ strategy _____ for the following reasons:

_____

_____

_____

Compare your answer with that of the author on page 63.

CHAPTER 9

The Contributions of Others Make You a Good Supervisor

The need to delegate

Delegating is the assignment of tasks and responsibilities to help employees make their best contribution to the overall productivity of your department. When you delegate you become a teacher. You tell an employee how to perform a new task effectively, show how it is done, and then ask that he or she demonstrate that the task has been learned. Delegating takes time, patience, and follow-up to ensure it is done correctly.

A supervisor must learn how to distribute tasks evenly, tap the special creativity of each individual and, when appropriate, rotate responsibilities among different employees. Proper delegation keeps employees motivated, increases productivity, and frees the supervisor for more important activities.

After setting a fair, consistent discipline line, the next big lesson is that you cannot do all the work yourself. You must delegate, and allow others to have responsibility to complete tasks which meet the expectations of your organisation. This means that intelligent delegation is more important than the actual work you do yourself. Building good relationships with employees helps to motivate them to do the work. It is a great thing for employees to like you, but respect is more important. These tips will help you to meet the second challenge. Tick each square as you go through the list.

☐ Nothing builds respect better than demonstrating to employees that you know what you are doing. Knowledge gives you power, and when you share it, you earn respect. Teach those who work for you everything you know to help them become more efficient.

☐ Set a good example. It is smart to pitch in and work from time to time to demonstrate your competence. But don't overdo it. Your skills are more valuable as a supervisor than as a worker.

☐ Create a relaxed but efficient working climate. People make mistakes and produce less when supervision is too close and constant. People should be able to enjoy their work within your discipline line.

☐ Circulate and communicate. Give your employees every opportunity to do a good job and when they do, follow up with compliments. Give credit freely when it is due.

☐ Keep an 'open door' policy. That is, be accessible to employees. Welcome their suggestions and complaints. If you set a discipline line that is too tight you will destroy the environment employees need to produce at an optimum level.

When Molly was only 20 years old, she became an instant supervisor without training. Although she was capable, enthusiastic, and did many things well, instead of delegating work Molly tried to do too much herself. As a result, she became ill through over-work and decided that supervision was not for her. Later, at 25 (after taking a course in beginning management), Molly had a second opportunity to be a supervisor. Realising that she would be judged by what her staff did (productivity) more than what she did herself, she delegated as much as possible so she would have extra time to build good relationships, communicate, and plan. Today, at 35, Molly is a successful executive and still developing.

CHAPTER 10
How to Delegate

Quality delegation takes planning. You must analyse all the tasks that need to be performed – before you start the process. Haphazard delegation can do as much harm as good.

Steps to take

A supervisor who learns to delegate effectively achieves two goals at the same time. First, more time is available to plan, organise and maintain relationships with other employees and co-workers. Second, employees become more versatile and valuable as they learn new tasks.

Below are ten typical steps in the delegating process. As you tick the list, assume you have been working overtime and need to hand over tasks you have been doing.

☐ **Step 1** Analyse your tasks and identify one you feel will provide you with additional freedom as well as benefiting the employee to whom you assign the responsibility.

☐ **Step 2** Select the most logical individual for the task you identify and delegate it. Be careful not to overload one employee.

☐ **Step 3** Instruct the individual selected how to perform the task. Do this in detail by both explaining and demonstrating. Explain why the task is important to the total operation.

☐ **Step 4** Solicit feedback to ensure the employee is prepared to assume the new responsibility. Provide opportunities for the employee to ask questions.

☐ **Step 5** Allow the employee you selected the freedom to practise the new assignment for a few days. Over-supervision can kill motivation.

☐ **Step 6** Follow up in a positive manner. When it is deserved, compliment the employee. If improvements are required, go through the instructions a second time.

☐ **Step 7** Consider the rotation of tasks: employees learn more and boredom is less likely when this is done. Also, an objective productivity comparison is possible among employees.

☐ **Step 8** Delegate those assignments which prepare employees to take over in the absence of others – including yourself.

☐ **Step 9** Give everyone an opportunity to contribute. Solicit employee ideas. Use their special talents and abilities.

☐ **Step 10** Discuss new assignments and rotation plans with the entire group to obtain feedback and generate enthusiasm.

CHAPTER 11
Become an Effective Counsellor

If you are a sports fan, you know the primary job of a coach is to build a cohesive team. When everyone works together the team is more likely to win. Personality conflicts can destroy a team. They can also destroy productivity in a department. A supervisor is a coach. She or he must keep harmony among workers to ensure productivity and win the game. The best way to do this is through good communication and counselling.

Counselling is sitting down in a private setting for an open discussion with an employee. Sometimes it is to pay a sincere compliment; sometimes it is to solve a problem that is reducing productivity; sometimes it is because an employee has violated company discipline and you need to give a warning. There are many counselling skills. One of the most important is being a good listener. This will help you to find the *real* problem, and then help the employee to make a mutually rewarding decision. There is no magic to good counselling. Anyone can do it.

We communicate on several levels from individual to large groups. We also communicate both formally and informally. When you become a supervisor, communication of all types, at all levels, takes on new importance.

Communicating one to one, in private, is counselling or interviewing. Once you become a supervisor you will discover that counselling is one of the best 'tools' you possess. Until you understand what counselling can do for you, it will be difficult to move to the next stage.

Below are ten situations. Seven call for admonition by the supervisor; three do not. Tick the three that require no counselling. Check your answers with those given at the bottom of the following page.

☐   1. An employee violates your standards.

☐   2. An employee is consistently late or absent.

☐ 3. You disagree with an employee's lifestyle.

☐ 4. An employee's productivity is down.

☐ 5. One employee behaves in such a way that the productivity of others is reduced.

☐ 6. You are upset.

☐ 7. Two employees have a conflict that is becoming public.

☐ 8. You dislike the personality of an employee.

☐ 9. You want to compliment an individual.

☐ 10. You want to delegate a new task.

If productivity in a department drops, action needs to be taken quickly. Time will not normally solve problems that must be addressed. Often action can take the form of counselling – either individual or group, or both.

It is important to remember that individuals who become good line supervisors become candidates for middle and upper management positions. Those who demonstrate their skills in the minor leagues (supervision) are often promoted to the major leagues. In supervision, as in football, it is extremely important to get started on the right foot. If you weave the strategies and techniques of this book into your behaviour patterns, you will be preparing yourself for a higher-paying, more challenging management role. Do not make the mistake of saying to yourself that excellent supervision is simply common sense. It is much more than that. That is why you should regularly review the skills you are learning so that you know and practise all the skills of competence required to win the management game.

Answers to exercise 3, 6, 8

CHAPTER 12

Can Sylvia Keep Her Job as a Supervisor?

Case 3

Sylvia, without realising it, has been spending too much time on budget and administrative reports and not enough time communicating with her ten employees. As a result, morale is low, productivity is down and two good employees are thinking about submitting their resignations. Everyone feels frustrated and unappreciated. The situation is so bad that Sylvia's boss called her into his office and informed her: 'Sylvia, you have committed a cardinal sin by neglecting your employees in favour of other responsibilities. Instead of delegating some of your work in order to free yourself, you locked yourself into your office and allowed things to fall apart outside. You could have great potential as a manager, but not until you learn to balance people activities with job tasks. You cannot have high productivity with low communication. All your employees feel you have been taking them for granted. A few have even talked to me about it. Your job as supervisor is in jeopardy. Be in my office at ten o'clock tomorrow with a plan to restore morale and productivity within ten days.'

What are Sylvia's chances of coming up with a plan that will turn things around?

Tick the appropriate box below and write out the reasons for your choice.

□	□	□	□
Excellent	Good	Long shot	Too late

_____

_____

Turn to page 63 to compare your answer with the author's.

CHAPTER 13
Become a Good Leader

To be highly effective as a supervisor you will want to put more leadership into your style. Everyone likes to work for a supervisor who keeps them motivated and headed in the right direction. Just as football players build loyalty towards coaches that lead them to victory, employees like supervisors who lead them to greater achievements.

Leadership means stepping out in front of others with new, workable ideas that save money and create greater productivity. Leadership means creating *followers* – employees who respect you to the point that they would like to follow you when you earn your next promotion. Becoming a supervisor is the best possible way to learn and practise leadership skills.

Your job as a supervisor is to establish departmental goals and then lead your people to achieve them. Keeping good records and ensuring that everyone stays busy is more management than leadership. Another way of saying it is that managing is the protection of what is already in place. Leadership, on the other hand, is reaching for new heights. Managers keep things the way they are to avoid trouble. Leaders take prudent risks to gain greater productivity. *You want to be a good manager, but you also want to be a leader.*

To become both – and get home safely – consider these tips:

First, be a good manager. Ensure that your operation is conforming to your organisation's standards. Watch details. Get reports in on time. Achieve the good feeling that comes from having everything under control.

Next, become a positive influence. Set new goals and motivate others to reach them. Stay positive. Keep things stirred up. Don't permit employees to become bored.

Help your people to reach their goals. Help them feel better about themselves. Provide the rewards and recognition they deserve. The better they feel about themselves, the more they will produce.

Now and then establish your authority. Employees need to be reminded that a discipline line exists. One way to demonstrate your authority is to make firm, difficult decisions. Another is to counsel disruptive employees and expect continued improvements in productivity.

Share good news. Keep the bad news in perspective. Look for positive things to talk about, including individual and group achievements. Make everyone feel that they are on a winning team.

CHAPTER 14
Provide Direction

Establish a productivity goal

'Management by objectives' is a system whereby supervisors submit their goals to higher management to be integrated with the organisation's goals. Supervisors are rewarded when their goals are achieved or surpassed.

Your organisation may not use this approach. If it does not, create your own goals (plans) on a weekly, monthly, and annual basis.

Those who set goals are usually more motivated to reach them. Even if management does not know about your goals (and consequently does not hold you accountable for reaching them) you will benefit from having them.

Everybody likes to be on a winning team. In your organisation, your department is a team which can win only if it reaches predetermined goals. *It is your responsibility as supervisor to help establish such goals and then motivate your people to reach them.*

Below are ten suggestions on how to motivate employees to reach a goal. Three are unacceptable because they will probably do more harm than good. Tick the squares opposite those that are counter-productive, and then compare your answers with those on page 39.

☐   1. Involve employees in setting goals.

☐   2. Make it easy for employees to motivate themselves by creating a relaxed and predictable working climate.

☐   3. At meetings, lay down the law. Tell everyone you are the boss, and things are to be done your way.

☐   4. Give employees credit when it is earned.

☐ 5. Circulate regularly and listen in order to discover the kind of rewards you can provide to improve productivity.

☐ 6. Act disappointed with everyone's performance as a method to get people to work harder.

☐ 7. Ask for suggestions from employees on how productivity can be improved.

☐ 8. Tell everyone that unless productivity improves their jobs are on the line.

☐ 9. Have a positive counselling session with each employee on a regular basis. Listen to complaints and, when possible, make adjustments to resolve the issue.

☐ 10. Through your own positive attitude create a more lively and happy work environment.

It is important that each member of a team shares in success. Communication is the only way this can happen.

Danger ahead

Gilbert is an outstanding producer, but he has a short fuse that often gets him into trouble. Maria is an excellent member of the department, but now and then she has a down period that requires great tolerance from her supervisor and co-workers. Craig is too chummy with all his co-workers but becomes upset when they prefer not to include him in their activities.

Q. With such characteristics, can Gilbert, Maria and Craig become successful supervisors?

A. Yes, but only if they can break those habits described above.

It is possible to tolerate such behaviour in an employee but it could spell disaster should the same behaviour surface in a supervisor.

After you hold down your job as a supervisor for about three months, you will start to feel comfortable with your new role.

However, you may need to change some habits before this happens.

If you are prone to make any of the mistakes listed in the following chapter, start to make corrections immediately or you will have trouble as a supervisor.

Answers to exercise 3, 6, 8

CHAPTER 15
Six Unforgivable Mistakes

1. Treating individuals unequally because of sex, culture, age, educational background etc. Each employee is unique and should receive the same consideration as any other.
2. Not keeping trust with an employee. The fastest way to destroy a relationship is to make a promise and then break it.
3. Blowing hot and cold. Consistency is essential when managing. If you are positive one day and down the next, employees will not know how to react. Respect will disappear.
4. Failure to follow basic company policies and procedures. As a line supervisor, you must handle your relationship with each employee in a fair and legal manner. This may mean, for example, establishment of an 'improvement plan' before you ask for approval to terminate an employee's appointment.
5. Losing your composure in front of others. Everyone reaches their threshold of tolerance on occasion but, as a supervisor, you need to keep your temper in check. Blowing up can destroy relationships.
6. Engaging in a personal relationship with someone you supervise. When you become a supervisor, you change your role. It is not possible to be in charge of a person during the day and personally involved with them after work.

As concisely as possible, in your own words, write the six unforgivable mistakes in the spaces below.

1. _____

2. _____

3. _____

4. _____

5. _____

6. _____

CHAPTER 16
Eliminating Personal Down Periods

Most of us are positive by nature, but many have serious trouble maintaining a positive attitude day in and day out. Sooner or later, negative feelings take over. This is more acceptable when you are an employee, but when you are a supervisor the consequences are more serious because you transmit your attitude to others. A poor attitude on your part can cause productivity to drop. Supervisors must put up a stronger battle to maintain a positive approach. It goes with the territory.

The responsibilities are often great and they can, without your realising it, turn you negative. The truth is, that when you are positive, productivity is up; but when you become negative, productivity drops. So your challenge is to remain positive even if those around you are not.

The exercise below assumes three things: (1) You are generally a positive, outgoing person. (2) There are certain things you can do to remain positive. (3) Being aware of these activities will assist you in the elimination of 'down periods'. After reading the list, select the three that will do the most for you.

☐ Engage in physical exercise of some sort.

☐ Give yourself more attainable goals.

☐ Try to take life less seriously.

☐ Share your positive attitude with others.

☐ Take more week-end or 'mini' vacations.

☐ Maintain a better balance between work and leisure.

☐ Improve your grooming.

☐ Do more to help others.

☐ Talk with a more experienced manager you respect to find a way to eliminate down periods.

Others:

_____

_____

_____

CHAPTER 17

Making the Transition Within the Same Department

If you are moving into your first assignment as a supervisor from being an employee in the same department, this programme has double significance. You will need to be highly sensitive because your fellow workers will observe and talk about you.

- Stay warm and friendly but slowly back away. You can't be too friendly *and* a supervisor at the same time.
- Do not permit those who were co-workers yesterday to intimidate you today. If you play favourites you are in trouble.
- Do what you can to make everyone's job better than it was before you became supervisor. Do not make the same mistakes your boss made when you were an employee.

Provide reinforcement

Employees like to know how they are doing. Take a few minutes every now and then to let your people know you appreciate their dependability and the contribution they are making. Many capable employees resign because superiors take them for granted.

You are only as good as the people who work for you. Make sure your employees regularly receive the reinforcement they need.

CHAPTER 18
Reacting to the Problem Employee

All supervisors must occasionally deal with a difficult or problem employee. Some employees are consistently late or absent from work – others create false rumours that affect the productivity of workers; still others fail to follow safety rules or make mistakes that need to be corrected. In extreme cases, problem employees carry hostility towards another employee or his or her supervisor.

How you deal with such employees and convert them into 'team members' is a critical part of your job. The following suggestions are designed to provide you with the help you may need.

Below are ten ways to react to an employee who is demanding, hostile and disruptive. Three are acceptable forms of behaviour. Tick the box opposite those you feel are appropriate behaviour for a supervisor, then match your answers with those at the bottom of the following page. Remember, we are talking about your initial reaction – not action that might be taken later.

☐ 1. Scowl, then inform the employee you consider him or her to be a problem.

☐ 2. Stare the employee down by silently challenging her or him with your eyes.

☐ 3. Stay cool. Let the employee express anger without an immediate reaction on your part.

☐ 4. Consider the employee as objectively as possible and refuse to take things personally.

☐ 5. Avoid the problem by walking away.

☐ 6. Become distant and uncommunicative.

☐ 7. Challenge the employee to stop giving you a problem.

☐   8. Act uninterested and ignore the situation.

☐   9. Get angry and give back the kind of behaviour you receive.

☐ 10. In a calm manner say: 'Let's talk in my office.'

Firm, friendly, and fair are the key words in maintaining your discipline line. But when a difficult situation arises, it is time to use your counselling skills.

To be an effective supervisor you need to know how to *create* and repair relationships with members of your staff. Good relationships are created when you:

- Provide clear, complete instructions.
- Let employees know how they are doing.
- Give credit where credit is due.
- Involve people in decisions.
- Remain accessible.

The best way to repair a relationship is through counselling.

CHAPTER 19
Will MRT Counselling Work?

Case 4

Kathy learned about MRT counselling last week. As she understands it, the idea is to sit down with a problem employee and discuss rewards she can provide for that employee, as well as rewards that employee can provide for her. The technique is based on the Mutual Reward Theory (MRT) which states that a relationship between two people can be enhanced when there is a satisfactory exchange of rewards between them. When the exchange is considered balanced, both parties will come out ahead.

Kathy has been having trouble with George for over a month. In desperation, she decides to call him into her office and discuss the situation to see if the Mutual Reward Theory can be applied. Her hope is that she can give him what he wants in exchange for a better attitude on his part.

Kathy starts the counselling session by complimenting George on his consistent productivity and asking him to suggest any rewards she is not providing that are within her capacity. She informs George that she will, in turn, suggest three rewards she would like to receive from him.

Here are George's suggestions:
1. More opportunity to learn.
2. More recognition.
3. Less supervision by Kathy.

Kathy in turn asks for the following:
1. Continued high productivity.
2. More cooperation with co-workers.
3. Less hostility towards herself.

George and Kathy spend 30 minutes discussing the rewards each wants and how the other could provide them. George admits that he could be more cooperative; Kathy admits that she can provide George with more opportunity to learn and they discuss a number of ways this can be accomplished.

Will this kind of MRT counselling work for Kathy? Will it permanently improve the relationship between Kathy and George? Write your answer in the space below and compare it with that of the author on pages 63–4.

_____

_____

_____

CHAPTER 20
Summary

Throughout this book you have learned that becoming a successful supervisor is a combination of many personal characteristics (positive attitude, personal confidence, patience etc) and the application of many tested skills and techniques (delegating, counselling, restoring relationships etc).

CAN YOU PUT ALL OF THESE REQUIREMENTS TOGETHER?

Of course you can – especially if you don't try to do everything at once! Keep in mind that, after all is said and done, the key to your success as a supervisor is how well you achieve improved productivity.

If your department is regularly noted for higher productivity than similar departments, your superiors will recognise this and you will be in a good position for future advancement.

Achieving greater productivity is a *human challenge*. As a supervisor, it is not what you can accomplish by doing tasks yourself but the quality of the working relationships you build with the people *who do the work for you*.

CHAPTER 21
Develop Your Human Skills

As an employee, your productivity was measured and compared with your co-workers'. Your superior normally did this through some kind of formal appraisal. Your promotion may have depended on these appraisals.

When you become a supervisor, you are measured by the productivity of your department or section. This means your future depends on how well your team performs. If you employ the human skills which motivate your staff to produce more, you will be recognised for doing a good job. If the opposite happens, your job may be in jeopardy.

It helps to contribute to productivity by doing a small amount of work yourself. This also helps to set the work pace. If you do too much yourself, however, your people may not get the supervision which will allow them to produce more.

To test your understanding, answer the following true and false questions. The correct answers are given overleaf.

True   False

——— ——— 1. Nothing should receive higher priority than helping an employee to reach his or her productivity potential.

——— ——— 2. A drop in productivity by a reliable employee need not be dealt with immediately as it might cause resentment.

——— ——— 3. Employees will often produce more for one supervisor than for another.

——— ——— 4. A disruptive employee who reduces the productivity of co-workers must be dealt with immediately.

——— ——— 5. Some employees with modest personal productivity can help the productivity of others so much that they are highly regarded by supervisors.

____ ____ 6. Most employees have higher productivity potential than they realise.

____ ____ 7. Generally speaking, the more employees produce, the better they feel about themselves.

____ ____ 8. Human skills are easier to learn than technical skills.

____ ____ 9. A clever supervisor can do less personally and still have the highest producing department.

____ ____ 10. A 'golden' employee is one who produces at a high level and, also, contributes measurably to the productivity of co-workers.

Make this your personal success formula

You can build your supervisory style around the formula on the next page. It contains all the basic ingredients required for success. You may tear or cut it out and paste it on your refrigerator or mirror as a reminder. It will help you to become comfortable and secure in your new role.

CHAPTER 22
Success Formula for Supervisors

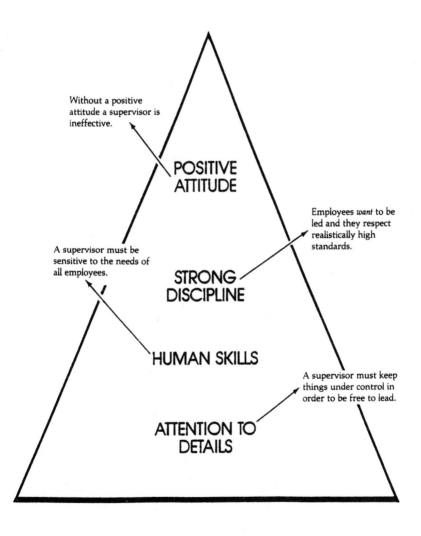

Without a positive attitude a supervisor is ineffective.

POSITIVE ATTITUDE

Employees *want* to be led and they respect realistically high standards.

A supervisor must be sensitive to the needs of all employees.

STRONG DISCIPLINE

HUMAN SKILLS

A supervisor must keep things under control in order to be free to lead.

ATTENTION TO DETAILS

Progress report

It is now time to measure the progress you have made. On the following page there are 20 statements. They are either true or false. Each correct answer is worth 5 points.

Answers will be found on page 58.

CHAPTER 23
Demonstrate Your Progress

For each statement below, put a tick under true or false.

True *False*

____ ____ 1. To make maximum use of this programme you should review it regularly.

____ ____ 2. *The Fifty-Minute Supervisor* should be considered as the first phase of a more extended supervisory training programme.

____ ____ 3. One way to become a successful supervisor is to do more of the actual work yourself.

____ ____ 4. Supervisors have less freedom than those they supervise.

____ ____ 5. Behavioural changes are not necessary for most people to become good supervisors.

____ ____ 6. Supervisors need not communicate a strong image.

____ ____ 7. You make a good start when you establish and maintain a fair and consistent discipline line.

____ ____ 8. Popularity is more important to the new supervisor than earning respect.

____ ____ 9. In setting a discipline line, it is better to start easy and get tough later.

____ ____ 10. It is easier to become a good supervisor when you are promoted within the same department.

____ ____ 11. Most supervisors are good at delegating.

____ ____ 12. Intelligent delegating takes too much time to be worthwhile.

____ ____ 13. Supervisors should remonstrate only as a last resort.

____ ____ 14. Most supervisors are better at managing than leading.

_____ _____ 15. Supervisors who stay in the background and control with a firm hand are usually the most successful.

_____ _____ 16. Coaching and counselling are not important enough to be two of the four basics in the football analogy.

_____ _____ 17. Counselling is the best technique for working with a problem employee.

_____ _____ 18. Unlike employees, a supervisor does not have the luxury of reporting to work in a negative mood.

_____ _____ 19. Failure to keep a promise to an employee is not an unforgivable mistake.

_____ _____ 20. Supervisors cannot afford to show compassion for employees.

| | TOTAL   See below for answers.

Answers to exercise

1. T Highly recommended.
2. T Hopefully you will be able to attend management seminars at a later date.
3. F A supervisor should _supervise_, not do actual work all the time.
4. F Supervisors have more freedom, especially if they learn how to delegate.
5. F Many behavioural changes are usually necessary.
6. F A stronger image is necessary but, of course, it should not be introduced too quickly or overdone.
7. T (See page 23.)
8. F
9. F Just the opposite; start out with a firm but fair line and relax to the proper point later.
10. F Just the opposite.
11. F

12. F It takes time at the beginning but releases time in the future.
13. F Counselling is a tool that can be used daily.
14. T
15. F Constant communication through circulation is required.
16. F Coaching and counselling constitute a basic supervisory tool.
17. T
18. T If the supervisor is down the entire team may be.
19. F
20. F There is nothing incompatible about being compassionate and still maintaining a strong, productive discipline line.

CHAPTER 24
Looking Ahead

Your score indicates the progress you have made thus far.

How can you become so successful as a line supervisor that you will have an opportunity to move higher? Here are three tips:

1. Regularly review the basics presented in this programme.
2. Discuss your successes and failures as a new supervisor with your superior. Learn from your mistakes.
3. Study other materials, attend seminars, become a 'student' of management and leadership.

Author's Suggested Answers to Cases

Who Will Survive?
It is the opinion of the author that both Joe and Mary will survive, but the edge is with Mary. Joe will probably be better liked as a supervisor. Mary, however, will probably earn more respect. Joe ignores the fact that there are many sound techniques and principles every supervisor should learn. He will survive only if he learns them in time.

Which Strategy Should Henry Use?
The author favours strategy 2 but would, also, follow up the group session with individual counselling to avoid any misunderstandings and improve relationships. Henry should not expect 100 per cent compliance with his new standards quickly. He should, however, set his standards high enough to achieve the kind of productivity desired. Reachable standards are required, but employees should be given sufficient time to attain them. While doing this, Henry should also set a good example both as a supervisor and worker.

Can Sylvia Keep Her Job as a Supervisor?
It is doubtful that Sylvia can turn things round. In fact, in similar situations, many experienced managers would transfer Sylvia to a non-supervisory position until she can demonstrate she is ready to assume the full responsibility of being a supervisor. Sylvia's boss is right in saying she committed a cardinal sin. The only way a supervisor can increase or maintain productivity is to establish and nurture good relationships with all employees. Once other activities take priority, morale begins to fall and trouble starts. Restoring relationships at this point is a long shot. Once relationships have deteriorated to a certain point, rebuilding them is almost impossible.

Will MRT Counselling Work?
If both Kathy and George make a serious effort to provide one or

more of the rewards wanted but not previously provided, the chances are excellent that the relationship will improve. MRT counselling frequently works because it opens up communication and both parties accept that there is something specific to do to make improvements. Care should be taken to announce in advance that there may be some rewards (such as an increase in pay) over which the supervisor does not have jurisdiction or complete control.

Further Reading from Kogan Page

Don't Do, Delegate! The Secret Power of Successful Managers, James M Jenks and John M Kelly, 1986

Essential Management Checklists, Jeffrey P Davidson, 1987

A Handbook of Management Techniques, Michael Armstrong, 1986

How to Be an Even Better Manager, Michael Armstrong, 1988

How to Develop a Positive Attitude, Elwood N Chapman, 1988

How to Make Meetings Work, Malcolm Peel, 1988

Profits from Improved Productivity, Fiona Halse and John Humphrey, 1988

Readymade Business Letters, Jim Dening, 1986

Winning Strategies for Managing People: A Task Directed Guide, Robert Irwin and Rita Wolenik, 1986